Bridgestone BOOKS

World of Insects

Dragonflies

by Deirdre A. Prischmann

Consultant:
Gary A. Dunn, MS, Director of Education
Young Entomologists' Society, Inc.
Minibeast Zooseum and Education Center
Lansing, Michigan

Capstone
press

Mankato, Minnesota

Bridgestone Books are published by Capstone Press,
151 Good Counsel Drive, P.O. Box 669, Mankato, Minnesota 56002.
www.capstonepress.com

Library of Congress Cataloging-in-Publication Data
Prischmann, Deirdre A.
    Dragonflies by / Deirdre A. Prischmann.
        p. cm.—(Bridgestone Books. World of insects)
    Summary: "A brief introduction to dragonflies, discussing their characteristics, habitat, life cycle,
and predators. Includes a range map, life cycle illustration, and amazing facts"—Provided by publisher.
    Includes bibliographical references and index.
    ISBN 0-7368-4337-X (hardcover)
    1. Dragonflies—Juvenile literature. I. Title. II. Series.
QL520.P75 2006
595.7'33—dc22   2004028519

Editorial Credits

Shari Joffe, editor; Jennifer Bergstrom, set designer; Biner Design, book designer;
    Patricia Rasch, illustrator; Jo Miller, photo researcher; Scott Thoms, photo editor

Photo Credits

Art Directors/Jim Ringland, 10
Bill Johnson, 12
Bruce Coleman Inc./Kim Taylor, 4
Corel, 1
KAC Productions/Larry Ditto, cover
Minden Pictures/Jim Brandenburg, 16
Pete Carmichael, 20
SuperStock, 6, 18

1 2 3 4 5 6 10 09 08 07 06 05

Table of Contents

Dragonflies 5

What Dragonflies Look Like 7

Dragonflies in the World 9

Dragonfly Habitats 11

What Dragonflies Eat 13

Eggs and Nymphs 15

Molting into an Adult 17

Dangers to Dragonflies 19

Amazing Facts about Dragonflies 21

Glossary 22

Read More 23

Internet Sites 23

Index 24

Dragonflies

Dragonflies are ancient insects. Their relatives were around before dinosaurs. Unlike dinosaurs, dragonflies still live in the world. Dragonflies have not changed much since ancient times.

Like all insects, dragonflies have six legs and an **exoskeleton**. The exoskeleton supports and protects the insect's body.

Dragonflies are closely related to damselflies. Damselflies are smaller. They hold their wings up when they rest. Dragonflies rest with their wings spread out.

◀ Dragonflies have been on earth for more than 320 million years.

What Dragonflies Look Like

Adult dragonflies often have colorful wings and bodies. Some dragonflies are smaller than a quarter. Others are longer than a dollar bill.

Dragonfly bodies have three parts, called the head, **thorax**, and **abdomen**. The eyes, **antennae**, and mouthparts are on the head. Dragonflies have large eyes and good eyesight. Their antennae are small. Four wings and six legs connect to the thorax. The long abdomen holds the heartlike pump.

◄ Dragonflies have large wings. They are among the fastest flying insects.

Dragonfly Range Map

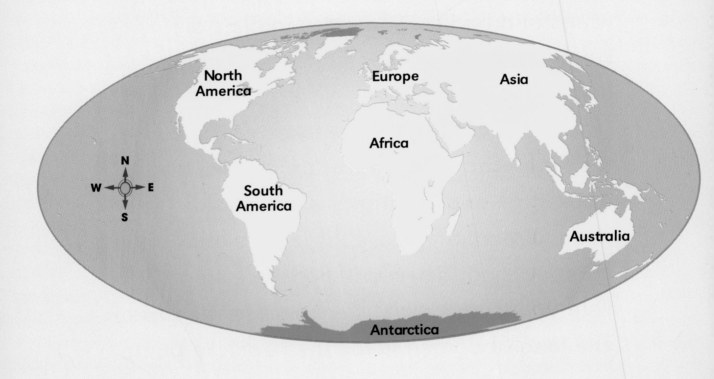

North America

Europe

Asia

Africa

South America

Australia

N
W · E
S

Antarctica

 Where Dragonflies Live

Dragonflies in the World

More than 2,000 kinds of dragonflies live around the world. More than 300 kinds live in North America.

Many dragonflies live where it is warm. Tropical forests have the most kinds of dragonflies. Some dragonflies live in deserts.

Dragonflies live in cold areas as well. They can be found in many parts of Alaska and in the Arctic Circle. Dragonflies also live high up in the mountains. They are not found in Antarctica.

Dragonfly Habitats

Adult dragonflies usually stay close to freshwater habitats. When not flying, dragonflies often rest on plants. Many males guard areas where they mate or where females lay eggs. These places are near the water's edge.

Young dragonflies, called **nymphs**, live in water or in wet areas. They can be found in ponds, lakes, or rivers. Some kinds of dragonfly nymphs live near waterfalls. Others are found on mosses or in muddy places.

◄ A dragonfly rests on a water plant.

What Dragonflies Eat

Adult dragonflies eat small flying insects. They usually catch their **prey** while flying through the air. Dragonflies have spines on their legs that help them grab and hold prey. Some kinds of dragonflies can snatch spiders from webs.

Nymphs eat water insects, tadpoles, and small fish. Nymphs have a mouthpart that adult dragonflies don't have. It is called a **labium**. A nymph quickly shoots out its labium to grab any prey that comes near.

◀ Dragonflies eat insects, including damselflies.

The Life Cycle of a Dragonfly

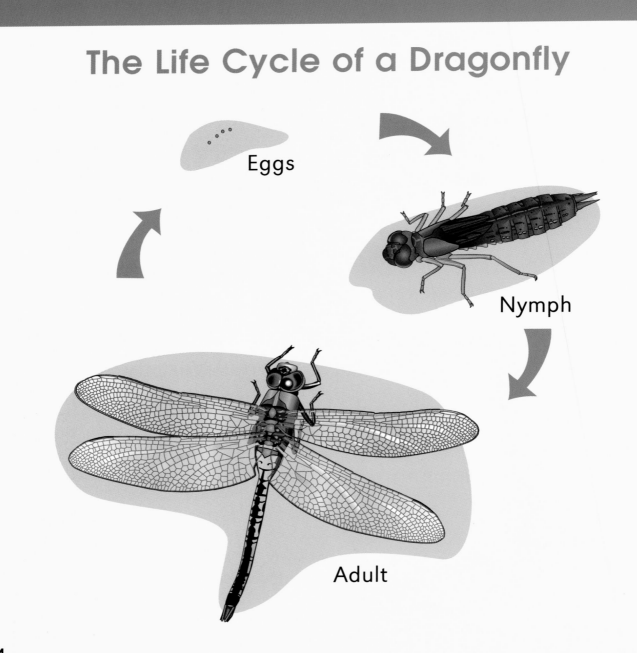

Eggs

Nymph

Adult

14

Eggs and Nymphs

Male and female dragonflies often mate while in the air. The male holds the female's head with his abdomen. The two dragonflies connect their bodies into a wheel shape. Many females also lay eggs while being held by the male.

Many dragonfly females put their eggs in or on plants. Some lay eggs in water. Most dragonfly eggs are oval. They may be white, grey, or yellow. Nymphs hatch from eggs after about one to three weeks.

Molting into an Adult

Nymphs look very different from adult dragonflies. They don't have wings and are usually dull brown or green.

Many dragonflies spend most of their lives as nymphs. The nymph stage lasts from three months to four years. As nymphs grow, they **molt**, or shed their exoskeleton, 8 to 15 times. The nymph's body changes with each molt. After the last molt, nymphs become adults with wings. Most adult dragonflies live for only one or two months.

◄ A new adult dragonfly stands near the nymph exoskeleton it has just molted.

Dangers to Dragonflies

Dragonflies have many **predators**. Birds, fish, and spiders eat adult dragonflies. Beetles and fish eat dragonfly nymphs. Dragonflies also eat each other. Some kinds of dragonflies hide from enemies by blending in with their surroundings.

People also harm dragonflies by destroying their habitats. Many kinds of dragonflies are now in danger of dying out. Dragonflies have been on earth for a long time. Hopefully, these amazing insects will not disappear.

◄ Birds are major predators of dragonflies.

Amazing Facts about Dragonflies

- Dragonflies have huge eyes that allow them to see in almost every direction. They can spot prey from 40 feet (12 meters) away.
- Ancient dragonfly relatives had wingspans of more than 2 feet (0.6 meters).
- Small animals called mites sometimes live on dragonflies. They suck the dragonflies' blood.
- Dragonflies can fly as fast as 38 miles (61 kilometers) per hour.

◄ Dragonflies have huge eyes and excellent vision.

Glossary

abdomen (AB-duh-muhn)—the end section of an insect's body

antenna (an-TEN-uh)—a feeler on an insect's head

exoskeleton (eks-oh-SKEL-uh-tuhn)—the hard outer covering of an insect

labium (LAB-ee-um)—the lower mouthpart of a dragonfly nymph

molt (MOHLT)—to shed an outer layer of skin, or exoskeleton, so a new exoskeleton can be seen

nymph (NIMF)—a young form of an insect; nymphs change into adults by molting several times.

predator (PRED-uh-tur)—an animal that hunts other animals for food

prey (PRAY)—an animal hunted by another animal for food

thorax (THOR-aks)—the middle section of an insect's body; wings and legs are attached to the thorax.

Read More

Jacobs, Liza. *Dragonflies.* Wild Wild World. San Diego: Blackbirch Press, 2003.

Kirkland, Jane. *Take a Walk with Butterflies and Dragonflies.* Lionville, Penn.: Stillwater Publishing, 2004.

Internet Sites

FactHound offers a safe, fun way to find Internet sites related to this book. All of the sites on FactHound have been researched by our staff.

Here's how:
1. Visit *www.facthound.com*
2. Type in this special code **073684337X** for age-appropriate sites. Or enter a search word related to this book for a more general search.
3. Click on the **Fetch It** button.

FactHound will fetch the best sites for you!

Index

abdomen, 7, 15
antennae, 7

body parts, 5, 7, 13, 17, 21

damselflies, 5
dangers, 19
defenses, 19

eating, 13
eggs, 11, 15
exoskeleton, 5, 17
eyes, 7, 21

food, 13

habitats, 9, 11, 19
head, 7, 15

labium, 13
legs, 5, 7, 13
life cycle, 15, 17

mating, 15
molting, 17
mouthparts, 7, 13

nymphs, 11, 13, 15, 17, 19

people, 19
plants, 11, 15
predators, 19
prey, 13, 21

range, 9

size, 7
speed, 7, 21

thorax, 7

wings, 5, 7, 17, 21